THERE IS STILL GOOD WE CAN DO

Reflections, Commentary, and Poems

2014 - 2024

Norman Hirsh

Copyright

Library of Congress
        Cataloging data

There Is Still Good We Can Do.
Hirsh, Norman.
1 – Poetry
2 – Spirituality
3 – Religious Criticism

ISBN: 9798330254965

10 9 8 7 6 5 4 3 2 1

Some of these poems have appeared in *The CCAR: A Reform Jewish Quarterly.*

For Peggy

Special thanks to my daughter, Sarah, for generously serving as my editor.

CONTENTS

INTRODUCTION

As I conclude this volume, at 94, I realize it is a gift of old age. Learning from *Psalm 90*: I number my days. I am more aware of eternity.

With thanks to God,
Norman Hirsh
June 2024

REFLECTIONS

Every single human being
on this earth is my
brother or sister.

-

To know as fully as possible
how much we do not know.

-

Realism is the road to patience.

-

Our task:
To grow from the
primitive toward the Eternal.

In a dark time:
do not forget there are beautiful things
in life and how much do I finally know?

-

It is a time of trial,
but there is still good we can do.

-

Kindness is caring, aware of need.

-

In retirement:
from rabbi
to poet
from being
to becoming,
goodness what I treasure
Torah what I study.

What one needs in life
is not a perfect solution,
but a way forward.

-

One day a week
we serve God
by not working.

-

I would like to discover
an immense quiet in myself
and from that quiet live my life.

-

There is sadness in life,
but don't give up joy.

I am reading two books:
one on World War II,
one on plum blossoms.
One tears me apart,
the other makes me whole.

-

Despite our death, the work we can do
here on earth is well worthwhile.

-

In one of the most difficult moments
of my life, this is what I heard
from deep within:
"No matter what happens,
you have to live a life
that counts for good."

-

The generations live in us,
and we live in the generations.

COMMENTARY

Psalm 16:8

"I have set the Lord always before me;
Surely He is at my right hand,
I shall not be moved."

Plain meaning:
stumble, fail to find safety,
fall before my enemies.
A midrash:
be moved away from my better self.

Genesis 1:31 in Old Age

"And God saw all that
He had made, and found it very good."

I had a friend
who looked out on his
much reduced world
and was able to say:
"It is very good."

Note:
For Jerry Gurland

Three Persistence Texts:

Genesis 32:27
"I (Jacob) will not let you go,
unless you bless me."

Exodus 17:12
emunah. "his (Moses') hands remained steady until the sun
set."

Ruth 3:10
chesed. "Your (Ruth) latest act
of kindness is even greater than the first…"

Note:
Translate *emunah* as steady faithfulness.
Translate *chesed* as loyal kindness.

G'vurot - Falling Not Fallen

someich noflim

Usual translation:
"supporting the fallen."
My translation:
"supporting the falling."

Noflim is a participle
expressing continuous action.
We are almost always
falling away from
our center of balance.

Note:
G'vurot is the second blessing
in the central prayer of our liturgy,
the Amidah. *G'vurot* speaks
of God's creative and helping
powers.

Calling Twice

God says to Moses (*Exodus 3:4*):
"Moses, Moses." God speaks the name twice.

Once, God addresses Moses as a man
of his time - the shepherd who sees
a strange sight in the wilderness.
The second call goes deeper so it
can enter the soul of Moses
and speak to the task that will
outlast his days.

God says to Abraham (*Genesis 22:1*):
"Abraham."

The voice reaches only the man of his time, an age of
child sacrifice.

But later the angel calls twice from heaven
(*Genesis 22:11*):
"Abraham, Abraham."

This time, the call penetrates the soul of Abraham,
the soul that loves his son.
This message we still hear today.

How can we, in our own way, call twice?

POETRY

A Life Can Be

Bach never finished
"The Art of the Fugue."

It grows in complexity
and beauty and then

suddenly stops,
but it doesn't end.

It remains,
A great work of creation,

like a life
which can become

more complex
deeper in goodness,

it stops,
but doesn't end.

Note:
Bach wrote "The Art of the Fugue" near the end of his
life and didn't finish it.

A Prayer for my Soul on my 88th Birthday

Flow gently to the shore,
grateful and with courage
if I can,
loving more,
less selfish by the end.

Flow gently to the shore,
thankful to those I love
and to Thee,
good deeds and sins,
I am at peace, mostly.

Lives touched,
a good name
left behind,
the Shema in my life,
the Shema on my lips,

Flow gently to the shore.

Winter Light

In the winter
without leaves
light grows
and slides away
through a pattern
of dark branches.

The First Plum Buds

Magenta
Soon the blossoms
Winter defied
Spring will come.

Blossoms and Branches

Our plum tree:
pale pink blossoms
criss-crossing dark branches,
no lessons:
only the gift
beauty brings.

Backyard in Early Spring

Winter is long,
patience not so long.

Plum trees blossom,
blossoms begin to fall.

The heart quiets.

Exile

We renewed passports.
We plan no trip.
Still, we may need to leave.
We are Jews.

Hearing the Cantor on Yom Kippur Afternoon

I saw myself
in a synagogue
a thousand years ago,
the same people
a similar melody
the same hope,
all of us together
in one moment
before God.

Unknown

There is no being
that is not becoming.
Life, death,
flowing falling rising
the heart of things
moves forward
it pierces the unknown,
we become
what we cannot be now.

A Brief Song, Welcomed

We each create a song with our lives,
it is brief,

but there is One
who welcomes this music

and passing all finitude
the song
remains

Immortality

We become part of
the endless river
of Your love
which binds
all things together.

Remembering

So often I mention the dead,
names dear to me,
precious because of their love
and what they brought to my life,
and I say
the traditional words
Alav hashalom
Aleha hashalom

For a moment they return
as an affirmation
that there is good
in this dark world

That one can become,
can even remain a blessing,
stronger than death
still a gift to life.

May my name be
recalled by a few
may they say
Alav hashalom.

Note:
Alav hashalom - Peace unto him
Aleha hashalom - Peace unto her

The Gift

It came to me I was rooted
in the unimaginable goodness of God.

I am grounded, I know,
in other soil, darker
than I want to think,
but I was joyful,
and decided
to anchor myself more firmly,
my soul reaching down
into the endless
love of the Creator.

Hoping to find
fresh energy to be kind,
a covenant with justice that endures,
the wisdom to be more accepting in my love,
an urgency to act in time.

Hoping to find a way,
patient effort,
then came the sudden gift of the Ultimate,
a goodness far deeper than my own,
rising into my life.

Thoughts Before My 92nd Birthday

Before I leave:
be faithful to a hope that is far off,
live a truth I make my own,
hold a hand I never want to let go,
embrace those I love,
and release when I must

be grateful
for the gift of each day,
forgive knowing human limits,
be forgiven
love can be deep

regret my sins
but hope I have done my duty,
find a way back
which is a way forward

let my motto be: there is still good I can do

believe there is a purpose
even if I do not know it -
perhaps, in part,
because I do not know it

be a moment embraced by the Eternal,
be a particle of dust

reaching toward the Infinite

know there is the almost Unknown
illuminated by love,
and we are unendingly
a part
of the Mystery.

A song we sing,
a deed we do.

And when my time comes:

Sleep, life has been good.
Now, let go.

Notes:
"be a particle of dust"
See Genesis 2:7: "The Lord God formed man from the
dust of the earth"

"the almost Unknown"
See Exodus 3:13-14: "I am that I am."

"illuminated by love"
See Exodus 34:5-7: "a God compassionate and gracious"

Near the End

Plum blossoms:
I was surprised to see
more than a few
sparkling
white
among the dying pink.

Rosh Hashanah 5784

Rosh Hashanah arrives,
death looms, disasters lie in wait,
"Remember us unto life."

I am with my people,
strength steadies,
goodness makes a stand,
"Today is the birthday of the world."

Rosh Hashanah to Yom Kippur,
the ten days of repentance,
judgment descends on me,
creation rises in me.

God moves to the throne of mercy,
I am forgiven.
I begin again.

Note:
In Jewish tradition, God is said to move from the throne
of justice to the throne of mercy.

After My Death

Does nothingness follow me
or some new ascent of my life,
some new closeness to truth?

Will I discard my map,
come nearer to who I am,
journey in the Mind of God?

I cannot know, but
love, goodness and
my loved ones go on.

Whatever God's plan,
summon a grateful yes.

Also By Norman Hirsh

Philosophy

Ethics and Human Relationships

Poetry

God Loves Becoming
Unfolding Toward Purpose